COVID-19 and Other Pandemics:
A COMPARISON

Don Nardo

ReferencePoint
Press®

San Diego, CA

© 2021 ReferencePoint Press, Inc.
Printed in the United States

For more information, contact:
ReferencePoint Press, Inc.
PO Box 27779
San Diego, CA 92198
www.ReferencePointPress.com

LIBRARY OF CONGRESS CATALOGING-IN-PUBLICATION DATA

Names: Nardo, Don, 1947- author.
Title: COVID-19 and other pandemics : a comparison / Don Nardo.
Description: San Diego : ReferencePoint Press, 2020. | Includes
   bibliographical references and index.
Identifiers: LCCN 2020043179 (print) | LCCN 2020043180 (ebook) | ISBN
   9781678200428 (library binding) | ISBN 9781678200435 (ebook)
Subjects: LCSH: Epidemics--History--Juvenile literature. | COVID-19
   (Disease)--Juvenile literature. | Diseases and history--Juvenile
   literature.
Classification: LCC RA643 .N36 2020 (print) | LCC RA643 (ebook) | DDC
   614.5/92414--dc23
LC record available at https://lccn.loc.gov/2020043179
LC ebook record available at https://lccn.loc.gov/2020043180

Contents

MAJOR PANDEMICS IN HISTORY

Name	Time period	Death toll
Antonine Plague	165–180	5 million
Plague of Justinian	541–542	30–50 million
Japanese Smallpox Epidemic	735–737	1 million
Black Death	1347–1351	200 million
New World Smallpox Outbreak	1520–	56 million
Great Plague of London	1665	100,000
Italian Plague	1629–1631	1 million
Cholera Pandemics 1–6	1817–1923	1 million+
Third Plague	1885	12 million (China / India)
Yellow Fever	Late 1800s	100,000–150,000 (US)
Russian Flu	1889–1890	1 million
Spanish Flu	1918–1919	40–50 million
Asian Flu	1957–1958	1.1 million
Hong Kong Flu	1968–1970	1 million
HIV/AIDS	1981–present	25–35 million
Swine Flu	2009–2010	200,000
SARS	2002–2003	770
Ebola	2014–2016	11,000
MERS	2015–present	850
COVID-19	2019–present	*1.4 million+

Johns Hopkins University estimate as of November 30, 2020*

Note: Many of the death toll numbers are best estimates based on available research.

Based on Nicholas LePan, "Visualizing the History of Pandemics," Visual Capitalist, March 14, 2020. www.visualcapitalist.com.

Learning the Lessons of Past Pandemics

In April 2020 people living near a Brooklyn, New York, funeral home were besieged for several weeks by the sickening smell of decomposing corpses. As the COVID-19 outbreak worsened by the day, New York's morgues and funeral homes were overwhelmed by the growing number of bodies of people killed by the disease. More than sixteen thousand New Yorkers had already died of the contagion, and more continued to perish.

The question for the employees of the Brooklyn funeral home was what to do with the corpses piling up around them. In desperation, they started stacking them in large, metal U-Haul trucks parked on a nearby street. It did not take long for the police to catch on, and they found not only the U-Haul trucks but also piles of bodies in two refrigerated trucks. Moreover, investigative reporters around the nation discovered that the same gruesome practice was happening in several other American cities.

The Morbid Universality of Disease

Many Americans who heard reports of these desperate measures assumed such horrors were new and unprecedented. But they were mistaken. In fact, the dilemma of what to do with fast-rising piles of human

Overwhelmed by casualties of COVID-19, in April 2020 health workers load bodies of the disease's victims into a refrigerated truck parked outside a funeral home in Brooklyn, New York.

bodies during large disease outbreaks is quite literally as old as humanity itself.

Archaeologists demonstrated this sad reality quite starkly when in 2011 they unearthed a five-thousand-year-old village in northwest China. Among the several huts excavated was one that contained the remains of ninety-seven bodies of men, women, and children. These individuals had apparently succumbed to some sort of disease, and their bodies had been jammed together inside the dwelling. Overwhelmed by the sheer number of corpses, both ancient and modern people essentially settled on the same solution.

Though separated by millennia, the similar reactions to onslaughts of deadly diseases illustrates that such outbreaks are not uncommon in history. It is a reminder that large attacks of lethal germs are nothing new, nor are human reactions to them. One problem inherent in such pandemics is that over time people tend to forget the lessons of the past. In the words of popular science writer Richard Conniff:

Epidemics always have afflicted humans, and pandemics since we first sprawled across the globe. They have taught us important lessons—if only we could manage to remember them in our exhaustion and relief after danger has passed us by. New pandemics such as COVID-19 have a way of reminding us how easy it is for us to infect one another, especially those we love. How fear of contagion forces us apart. How devastating isolation can be, and yet how the sick often must die miserably and alone.[1]

In his comments, Conniff makes a distinction between the terms *epidemic* and *pandemic*. An epidemic is generally defined as a large outbreak of a certain disease in a given, confined geographic area. In contrast, a pandemic is a very large-scale epidemic that affects a much larger area, such as an entire continent or the world in general. In his popular book about pandemics, medical researcher Peter C. Doherty states, "A novel infection—new and previously unconfronted—that spreads globally and results in a high incidence of morbidity (sickness) and mortality (death) has, for the past 300 years or more, been described as a pandemic."[2]

> ## By the NUMBERS
>
> Experts today estimate that 2 million to 8.7 million people died in the 1817 cholera pandemic that began in Calcutta, India.

Witnesses to Past Pandemics

The diseases that spark pandemics can be devastating not only for the victims but also for the people around them. This, as Conniff points out, was the case with the cholera pandemic that began in northeastern India in 1817 and then spread into most other parts of Asia. The initial cause of the pandemic was contaminated rice. Those who ate it soon fell ill and then died a horrible death. "It wasn't just that it killed half its victims and did so with appalling speed," Conniff says, describing in detail the ghastly progression of the disease:

A special horror attended the way they died, with a person who was in the prime of life one moment seeming, in the next, to liquify and flow out in uncontrollable vomiting and diarrhea. Intense thirst followed. Spasms and cramps wrenched the muscles. Breathing became a desperate, gasping "air hunger." Victims died with their minds seemingly intact, staring, aghast, the watery liquid still being wrung from their guts.[3]

Much of what is known about past pandemics comes from the written accounts and descriptions of people who lived through these events. One of the more valuable of such accounts for modern researchers is a surviving letter penned in 1562 by an English nobleman, Lord Randolph. Part of his description of Mary, Queen of Scots's bout with influenza—or the flu—states, "She fell acquainted with a new disease that is common in this town . . . which passed also through her whole court, neither sparing lords, ladies, nor damsels. [It] is a plague in their heads that have it, and a soreness in their stomachs, with a great cough. . . . The queen kept [to] her bed six days."[4]

Today a massive worldwide media exists, the size of which would have astounded people in Queen Mary's day. Thousands of modern written and photographic sources are recording for posterity the symptoms and social consequences of the deadly COVID-19 pandemic. Whether the world would come together in a concerted effort to defeat this disease remained uncertain throughout much of 2020. As the Canadian University of Waterloo scholar Thomas Homer-Dixon says, the COVID-19 pandemic should "remind us of our common fate on a small, crowded planet. We won't address this challenge effectively if we retreat into our tribal identities. COVID-19 is a collective problem that requires global collective action."[5]

Chapter One

Pandemic Diseases in the Ancient Era

The exact nature of the first epidemics and pandemics are lost in the murky mists of time. Yet evidence suggests that people were periodically visited by disease outbreaks well before they dwelled in primitive huts in tiny villages. The precise origins of the many infectious sicknesses that have emerged over the ages are varied and mostly unknown. But as the late, great American historian William H. McNeill suggested, at least some of those maladies were initially transmitted to humans by fellow primates, particularly monkeys and great apes:

> Though important details remain unclear, the array of parasites that infest wild primate populations is known to be formidable. In addition to various mites, fleas, ticks, flies, and worms . . . among the organisms that infect monkeys and apes in the wild are fifteen to twenty species of malaria. Humankind normally supports only four kinds of malaria, but apes can be infected with human strains of malaria . . . and people can likewise suffer from some of the kinds of malaria found among monkeys and apes.[6]

Pulex irritans, *the so-called human flea, is seen here under magnification. Such fleas are known to bite mammals, including rats, mice, pigs, dogs, cats, bats, monkeys, and humans, and historically have spread deadly diseases, notably bubonic plague.*

More certain is that the effects of diseases on human populations worsened following the switch from hunting and gathering to settled agriculture, which occurred sometime between ten thousand and twelve thousand years ago. That watershed event in humanity's story significantly changed people's social habits, making contracting and spreading those illnesses easier. According to McNeill:

Settling down to prolonged or permanent occupancy of a single village site involved new risks of parasitic invasion. Increased contact with human feces as they accumulated in proximity to living quarters, for instance, could allow a wide variety of intestinal parasites to move safely from host to host. By contrast, a hunting band, perpetually on the move . . . would risk little from this kind of infectious cycle. We should expect that human populations living in sedentary communities were therefore far more quickly infested with worms and similar parasites than their hunting predecessors.[7]

Plagues in Civilization's Early Cradles

In the centuries following the emergence of farming and settled communities, the first large-scale civilizations appeared. They were nestled along the banks of large rivers in Mesopotamia (now Iraq), Egypt, India, and China, and modern historians call them the "cradles of civilization." In those and nearby areas, epidemics of certain diseases repeatedly returned in cycles, generating understandable fear among local populations. In the late 1300s BCE, for example, in ancient Hatti (land of the Hittites, part of what is now Turkey), a scribe wrote, "What have you done O Gods? You have allowed a plague to enter the land of Hatti and all of it is dying! Now there is no one to prepare food and drink offerings for you! No one reaps or sows the gods' fields, for the sowers and reapers are all dead! . . . The cowherds and shepherds are all dead!"[8]

The disease that caused that long-ago outbreak is unknown, as is that of another epidemic that struck China in the century that followed. A surviving Chinese document from the 1200s BCE worriedly asks, "Will this year have pestilence and will [there] be deaths?"[9] Meanwhile, the Hebrew Old Testament, composed in the Middle East in the first millennium BCE, is filled with references to diseases afflicting society. Typical is the warning that those who disobey God will suffer from such ailments in a passage from Deuteronomy: "The Lord will smite you with consumption [tuberculosis] and with fever, inflammation, and . . . [these ailments] will pursue you till you perish."[10]

The 430 BCE Athenian Plague

Very little detail about diseases and their symptoms in such early ancient epidemics has survived. The first large-scale disease outbreak that was extensively documented by a Greek historian was the so-called plague that struck the Greek city-state of Athens in the fifth century BCE. That historian was the Athenian chronicler Thucydides, who recorded the events of the devastating Peloponnesian War, fought between Athens and its archrival, Sparta. During that conflict, Thucydides writes, in the spring of 430 BCE the Spartans found an unexpected ally—a terrible disease that descended on the Athenians. By observing sick people, and also as a result of contracting the malady himself, the historian was able to concisely notate the painful symptoms in considerable detail. People who seemed to be in good health, he reports,

suddenly began to have burning feelings in the head. Their eyes became red and inflamed. Inside their mouths there was bleeding from the throat and tongue, and the breath became unnatural and unpleasant. The next symptoms were sneezing and hoarseness of voice, and before long, the pain settled on the chest and was accompanied by coughing. Next the stomach was affected, with stomachaches and with vomiting of every kind of bile. . . . The skin was rather reddish and livid, breaking out into small pustules [boils] and ulcers . . . and [later came] uncontrollable diarrhea.[11]

Some modern medical authorities say that several of these symptoms are similar to those of typhoid fever. Others have speculated that the Athenian plague was an early outbreak of either smallpox or measles. Whatever it actually was, the disease spread quickly through the crowded, walled city, and at least 20 percent of the population perished. Of the survivors, some went blind and many children were orphaned. In addition, the city-state's chief politician and military general, Pericles, died of the illness, leaving leaders of lesser quality to handle the double crisis of war and plague.

By the **NUMBERS**

Modern estimates place the Athenian plague's death toll at 75,000 to 100,000, or approximately 25 percent of the city-state's population.

An Overwhelming Catastrophe

In this passage from his riveting account of the epidemic that struck Athens in the spring of 430 BCE, Thucydides emphasizes two factors that are typical of disease outbreaks in cities. The first is overcrowding, which helps a disease spread; the second is the breakdown of various social norms and customs, caused by widespread fear and chaos.

A factor which made matters much worse than they were already was the removal of people from the country into the city [to take refuge from the attacking Spartans], and this particularly affected the incomers. There were no houses for them, and, living as they did during the hot season in badly ventilated huts, they died like flies. The bodies of the dying were heaped one on top of the other, and half-dead creatures could be seen staggering about in the streets or flocking around the fountains in their desire for water. The temples in which they took up their quarters were full of the dead bodies of people who had died inside them. For the catastrophe was so overwhelming that men, not knowing what could happen next to them, became indifferent to every rule of religion or of law. All the funeral ceremonies that used to be observed were now disorganized and they buried the dead as best as they could. . . . [Sometimes] they would throw the corpse they were carrying on top of another one and go away.

Thucydides, *The Peloponnesian War*, trans. Rex Warner. New York: Penguin, 1972, pp. 154–55.

Rome Ravaged by Smallpox?

Although clearly deadly, in both scope and death toll the Athenian epidemic of 430 BCE paled by comparison to a true pandemic that struck the Mediterranean world between 165 and 180 CE. Most of southern Europe, North Africa, and the Middle East were then parts of the Roman Empire. The residents of that realm suffered greatly from what eventually became known as the Antonine plague. It apparently emerged somewhere in China, spread steadily westward, and infected Roman soldiers who were then stationed in what is now Iraq. As large numbers of them subsequently returned home, they brought the contagion with them.

The famous Greco-Roman physician Galen examined victims of the plague in 166 and recorded its symptoms, among them fever, coughing, diarrhea, and ugly skin sores. About the latter, he observed that eventually, "that part of the surface called the scab fell away and then the remaining part nearby was healthy and after one or two days became scarred over."[12]

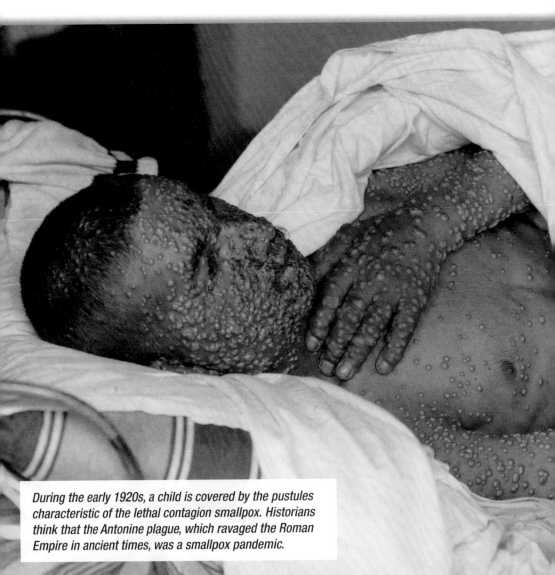

During the early 1920s, a child is covered by the pustules characteristic of the lethal contagion smallpox. Historians think that the Antonine plague, which ravaged the Roman Empire in ancient times, was a smallpox pandemic.

The disease was so infectious that at one point two thousand to five thousand people were dying each day in the city of Rome alone. In all, an estimated 5 million people died in the pandemic, some 10 percent of the Roman Empire's

population. That does not count all those who contracted the disease, however. Galen importantly noted that some sufferers survived their bouts with it and thereafter displayed immunity to it. Based on this and Galen's other descriptions, today a majority of medical experts think that the disease was likely smallpox.

The Whole Human Race Threatened?

Although the Roman realm managed to survive the pandemic, it had been severely weakened by it. Another similar blow to Roman civilization occurred not long after the western sector of its dominion collapsed in the late 400s CE. The eastern portion, centered at Constantinople, remained intact and over time mutated into the Byzantine Empire. The disease appeared in 541, during the reign of the Roman/Byzantine emperor Justinian, and for that reason it came to be known as the Justinian plague.

Justinian's chief court historian, Procopius, contracted the ailment himself but was among the fortunate individuals it did not kill. "The whole human race came near to being annihilated," he later wrote in his now famous description of the crisis. The victims, he continued,

had a sudden fever, some when just roused from sleep, others while walking about, and . . . the fever was of such a languid [tranquil] sort from its commencement and up till evening that neither to the sick themselves nor to a physician who touched them would it afford any suspicion of danger. It was natural, therefore, that not one of those who had contracted the disease expected to die from it. But on the same day in some cases, in others on the following day, and in the rest not many days later, a [roundish] swelling developed; and this took place not only in the particular part of the body which is called *boubon*, that is, "below the abdomen," but also inside the armpit, and in some cases also beside the ears, and at different points on the thighs.[13]

Based on this and other contemporary descriptions, modern doctors believe this was the first great pandemic caused by bubonic plague, which would later earn the nickname of the Black Death. The Justinian version may have been the largest, most destructive pandemic to strike humanity up to that point in history; it spread well into Europe, Asia, and Africa and killed at least 25 million people and possibly two or three times that many.

The social, economic, cultural, and political impacts of the Justinian plague, which struck in waves for many decades, were enormous. Indeed, in the words of Loyola University scholar J.N. Hays, the disruptions the pandemic caused "may have contributed to the transition between the ancient and medieval periods of Western history."[14] No less crucially, evidence suggests that due to these outbreaks, bubonic plague became well established in fleas that infested rats in some parts of Europe and beyond. This was destined a few centuries later to play a key role in what would prove to be Europe's worst pandemic ever.

Chapter Two

The Black Death Devastates Europe

"How shall I begin?" asked the fourteenth-century Italian scholar and poet Francesco Petrarca, popularly known as Petrarch, in a letter penned in early 1348. He went on to present a gripping description of the horrifying disease that came to be known as the Black Death, saying in part, "On all sides is sorrow; everywhere is fear. I would, my brother, that I had never been born. . . . When has any such thing been even heard or seen; in what annals has it ever been read that houses were left vacant, cities deserted, the country neglected, the fields too small for the dead, and a fearful and universal solitude over the whole earth?"[15]

Soon afterward, Petrarch's contemporary, Giovanni Boccaccio, recorded similar dark images of the death and destruction the plague wrought in Italy's great cultural center of Florence. "The city was full of corpses," he wrote. "Brother abandoned brother, uncle abandoned nephew, sister left brother, and very often wife abandoned husband, and—even worse, almost unbelievable—fathers and mothers neglected to tend and care for their children as if they were not their own."[16]

Widespread Damage

The Black Death struck Florence and a number of other Italian cities in 1348, after entering Europe from the east two years before. Disease epidemics had ravaged the continent in prior ages, but most had been confined to scattered individual regions. The Justinian plague of the 500s CE had been the main exception, but even that damaging outbreak could not match either the scale or ferocity of the Black Death. The latter reached almost every nation and city, killing thousands of people each and every day. In less than a decade, modern experts estimate, at least 25 million to 30 million souls perished in Europe alone (a third or more of the continent's population), and at least another 20 million to 30 million may have died in Asia and Africa.

The astounding death toll was only part of the widespread damage caused by the plague. Entire families, neighborhoods, and villages were wiped out. And unlike many debilitating diseases, which primarily kill society's most vulnerable people—the poor, children, and the elderly—the Black Death often attacked people in the prime of life. Yale university historian Frank M. Snowden explains the resulting horrific effects:

> This aspect made the plague seem like an unnatural or supernatural event. It also magnified the economic, demographic, and social dislocations that it unleashed. In other words, plague left in its wake vast numbers of orphans, widows, and destitute families. Furthermore, unlike most epidemic diseases, the plague did not show a predilection [preference] for the poor. It attacked universally.[17]

The result was that this great pandemic left Europe's plague survivors forever psychologically changed. Economic, social, and educational systems were also permanently altered, and many historians see this as the beginning of the complex, two-century-long transformation of medieval Europe into its early modern form.

Of these crucial changes, one of the most influential in Europe then and in later ages was a fundamental transformation of how members of the lower classes viewed their place in society.

Before the Black Death appeared, for instance, the commoners (most of whom were poor peasants) were under the strict economic and social control of the nobles and other wealthy citizens. But as the plague spread fear, chaos, and death, it became clear to all that the upper classes had been devastated as much as the lower ones. This realization made many of the surviving peasants feel emboldened. Daringly, they began defying their supposed "betters," for example, by demanding higher wages.

In turn, national and local rulers and other members of the upper classes reacted by trying to keep the commoners in their place, sometimes by forceful means. For example, some nobles forbade peasants to leave the rich estates on which they lived and worked for the owners. Other new rules

An illustration depicts residents in England burying plague victims in a mass grave in 1349. The bubonic plague, or Black Death, as it was known then, caused the creation of thousands of such mass burials all across Europe and beyond.

were meant to keep commoners who worked in shops from making higher wages. These and other measures strove to return society to the social and economic state it had been in before the onset of the plague.

Such oppressive tactics only served to anger and further embolden the peasants, who proceeded to stage uprisings of varied sizes and severity all across Europe. One of the largest occurred

Putting the Blame on the Jews

All sorts of theories about what caused the bubonic plague circulated through Europe during the 1300s. One of the meanest and most destructive was the vicious anti-Semitic charge that the malady was the result of Jews poisoning water supplies in order to kill Christians. According to a German Christian clergyman of that era, Heinrich Truchess von Diessenhoven, in November 1348 Jews in the German city of Sölden were burned to death because of a rumor they had poisoned local wells and rivers. Moreover,

> all the Jews between Cologne and Austria were burnt and killed for this crime, young men and maidens and the old along with the rest. And blessed be God who confounded the ungodly who were plotting the extinction of his church. . . . On 20 December in Horw, they [the Jews] were burnt in a pit. And when the wood and straw had been consumed, some Jews, both young and old, still remained half alive. The stronger of [the Christians] snatched up cudgels [clubs] and stones and dashed out the brains of those trying to creep out of the fire, and thus compelled those who wanted to escape the fire to descend to hell.

Quoted in Rosemary Horrox, ed., *The Black Death*. Manchester, UK: Manchester University Press, 1994, pp. 208–209.

England's King Richard II prepares to stop a local revolt. Unhappy over restrictive government rules related to the Black Death, across Europe groups of peasants burned the homes of wealthy and privileged people.

in France in 1358. The French chronicler Jean Froissart wrote that hundreds of armed commoners "went to the house of a knight dwelling thereby, and broke up his house and slew the knight and the lady and all his children great and small and burned his house."[18] As the rebels grew to number more than six thousand, they destroyed dozens of manor homes and slaughtered the occupants. A similar large peasant revolt occurred in England in 1381. Feeling threatened, King Richard II granted the peasants several concessions, including lowering their taxes.

Futile Attempts to Explain the Calamity

The Europeans whose society was in a sense turned inside out by the disease had no idea what was killing them by the millions.

In contrast, modern historians and medical experts have determined that it was the same contagion that had wreaked havoc during the Justinian pandemic—bubonic plague. Caused by a lethal bacterium called *Yersinia pestis*, it is principally a disease of wild rodents. Several writers of that era described the symptoms, at times in agonizing detail. One of them was Franciscan friar Michael of Piazza, whose account says in part:

> Boils developed in different parts of the body [including] on the sexual organs, in others on the thighs, or on the arms, and in others on the neck. At first these were the size of a hazelnut and the patient was seized with violent shivering fits [and] consumed by a violent fever. . . . Soon the boils grew to the size of a walnut, then to that of a hen's egg, or a goose's egg, and they were exceedingly painful, [causing the victim] to vomit blood.[19]

One of the scariest and saddest aspects of the plague's terrifying march through Europe was that no one knew how to stop it or to treat its victims. This is not surprising, considering that these events occurred more than five centuries before scientists learned of the connection between germs and disease. Still, some people did try to explain what was happening. The most common theory was that the pandemic was God's wrath. One Englishman wrote, "Plague is killing men and beasts. Why? Because vices rule unchallenged here."[20] In faraway Italy, meanwhile, Boccaccio called the crisis "God's just wrath as a punishment to mortals for our wicked deeds."[21]

Indeed, the plague caused a great many Europeans to begin questioning their long-held views of death, God, and life in general. No one seemed to have the power to halt the pandemic—not even God's chief human representatives, the priests. Their powerlessness led many to wonder whether the Almighty no longer cared what happened to the human race. Scholar Philip Ziegler, a noted expert on the Black Death, points out that fourteen-cen-

An Angry God or No God at All?

For many Europeans, the vast death and destruction wrought by the plague seemed to confirm that God was both real and angry with humanity. Yet in contrast, an undetermined number of people drew the opposite conclusion—that there might be no all-powerful deity at all. Yale University historian Frank M. Snowden explains:

> The plague in Europe led to an outpouring of sermons and religious pamphlets in which a central theme was theodicy—that is, the vindication [proof] of an omnipotent God's goodness in the face of evil and suffering. It was relatively easy to accept that God could be angry and would punish those who turned from Him and disobeyed His commandments. But how could one explain the gruesome suffering and mass death of innocents, especially children? It is true that the plague led to an upsurge of piety, but it also generated a powerful undertow pulling in the opposite direction. For some, the experience of bubonic plague led to the terrifying conclusion that there might be no God. A loving and all-powerful being would not take the lives of half the population of a great city, indiscriminately slaying men, women, and children. The result was not so much atheism, as a mute despair that was more often barely articulated—a psychological shock that, with historical hindsight . . . one might call post-traumatic stress.

Frank M. Snowden, *Epidemics and Society: From the Black Death to the Present.* New Haven, CT: Yale University Press, 2019, pp. 31–32.

tury Europeans endured a widespread "crisis of faith." He notes that "assumptions which had been taken for granted for centuries were now in question, [and] the very framework of men's reasoning seemed to be breaking up."[22]

Several other explanations were also advanced. One suggested the disease stemmed from "unclean" air. In October 1348 some French physicians claimed that "bad air is more noxious than food or drink in that it can penetrate quickly to the heart and lungs to do its damage."[23]

To their credit, some European doctors and scholars deduced that the plague was somehow contagious, even though they could not explain why. As a result, some towns instituted safety measures, including restricting travel, enforcing sanitary practices, and separating plague victims from healthy people. In March 1348, for instance, city officials in Venice supplied special barges to carry sick people to isolated islands. They also mandated that plague dead be buried at least 5 feet (1.5 m) deep. Though smart, these efforts ultimately proved futile because people remained ignorant of the primary danger—the infected fleas carried by the rats everywhere infesting human habitations.

A Wake-Up Call for Civilization?

Thus, the pandemic raged on, largely unimpeded, for three more years. By early 1351 it had begun to wind down, since far fewer people died that year than in the preceding few years. Nevertheless, bubonic plague was not yet finished with Europe, nor with other parts of the world. New eruptions of the disease occurred far and wide in subsequent centuries, including outbreaks in France in 1596, England in 1603, Russia in 1770, China in 1894, and the United States in 1900. However, none of these outbreaks compared in scope and lethality to the one that struck between 1346 and 1351.

The plague's great fourteenth-century visitation was also notable for its dramatic and far-reaching effects on the survivors and their descendants. Indeed, the social, technological, economic, and religious impacts of the Black Death were profound. One of the biggest changes it wrought was the collapse of the medieval manorial system, in which rich nobles dwelling in castles had exploited generations of poor peasants. Because millions of peasant workers died, workforces on the rich manors severely shrank. The work still needed to be done, of course, which gave the surviving peasants more leverage in their dealings with the nobles. All across Europe workers demanded and won the right to rent or even own parts of the fields they tilled. The result was a decrease in the power of the wealthy classes and a dramatic rise in the standard of living for members of the lower classes.

The Black Death also forever changed the way people viewed the Christian faith. Unable to stop the pandemic, many clergy members had suffered a loss of prestige. So, although most Christians remained devout believers, large numbers of them concluded that they could build a personal relationship with God without needing a priest as an intermediary.

Finally, the Black Death was widely seen as a sort of wake-up call. A large portion of the population came to believe that civilization *could* be totally destroyed, whether by God or natural forces. Therefore, they reasoned, people should never take concepts like prosperity, happiness, morality, or even life itself for granted. Indeed, society's collapse and humanity's demise could well be lurking just around the next corner. In Ziegler's words, after 1351 humanity moved forward into an uncertain future, "with one nervous eye always peering over its shoulder towards the past."[24]

Chapter Three

Conquest and Disease: The Columbian Plagues

The Antonine plague, Justinian plague, Black Death, and other large-scale disease outbreaks of the distant past have been covered in modern literature in as much detail as existing historical records allow. It is possible that their widespread coverage stems partly from the fact that these pandemics struck Europe. Not surprisingly, most of the major modern accounts of them were penned by Europeans or the descendants of Europeans.

In contrast, another historic pandemic—one of no less epic proportions and consequences—is covered in far less detail in modern accounts of the history of pandemics. Perhaps this is because the awful events in question were linked with Europeans' exploration and frequently brutal conquest of the Americas. "Between 1493 and the end of the sixteenth century," states J.N. Hays,

> the American continents suffered a repeated series of epidemics that had a catastrophic effect on their populations and civilizations. Those epidemics played a crucial role in the sudden and overwhelming conquests of the Americas by Europeans, and also in the vast movement of

Africans (as slaves) to the Americas. The sixteenth-century American epidemics therefore rank among the most decisive events of world disease history, and indeed of world history generally.[25]

To most people at the time, these sixteenth-century outbreaks appeared to be parts of one overriding, grand-scale pandemic. However, in reality they were caused by several different diseases, including smallpox, hemorrhagic fever, enteric fever, and others. Lumping them together, modern experts variously call the pandemic the New World plagues, American plagues, or Columbian plagues (after Christopher Columbus, whose followers were the first to bring disease germs from Europe to the Americas).

Italian navigator Christopher Columbus lands on an island in the West Indies. He was only the first of many European explorers and settlers who brought with them diseases that devastated local native populations.

Entire Societies Devastated

Unlike White Europeans, New World inhabitants had built up no immunity to Old World diseases. This made the indigenous peoples highly susceptible to contracting those maladies. As a result, these illnesses contributed heavily to the collapse of the Inca in South America and the Aztec, the Maya, and their neighbors in Central America. An estimated 90 percent of those indigenous populations were wiped out by the Columbian pandemic. "Whole societies fell apart," William H. McNeill writes, "values crumbled, and old ways of life lost all shred of meaning."[26]

A graphic description of the pandemic's effects on Central American native societies has survived in a 1571 tract penned by a descendant of Mayan royalty who as an adult took a Spanish name. It reads in part:

Great was the stench of death. After our fathers and grandfathers succumbed, half the people fled to the fields. The dogs and vultures devoured the bodies. The mortality was terrible. Your grandfathers died, and with them died the son of the king and his brothers and kinsmen. So it was that we became orphans, oh my sons! So we became when we were young. All of us were thus. We were born to die![27]

This idea—that local peoples were destined to die out because they were inherently inferior—became widespread among the Central American natives. A psychologically damaging belief, it grew from their perception that the Christian god was all-powerful and superior to their own deities. Seemingly confirming this view was the fact that the vast majority of White invaders consistently escaped the ongoing plagues that repeatedly devastated the indigenous nations. As McNeill points out:

Such partiality could only be explained supernaturally, and there could be no doubt about which side of the struggle enjoyed divine favor. The religions, priesthoods, and way of life built around the old Indian gods could not survive such a demonstration of the superior power of the god the Spaniards worshiped. Little wonder, then, that the Indians accepted Christianity and submitted to Spanish control so meekly. God had shown Himself on [the Spanish] side, and each new outbreak of infectious disease imported from Europe renewed the lesson.[28]

The Broken Spears

In spite of the onslaught of several different infectious diseases in the Americas in the 1500s, a majority of the fatalities overall were the result of smallpox. The disease is caused by a virus, and an infected person breaks out in a distinctive skin rash—the bump-like pox. In Europe and other parts of the Old World, roughly three out of every ten people who contracted the disease died. But having no natural immunity to it, the Native Americans' mortality rate was a good deal higher.

Smallpox's assault on the Americas began in 1492 when Columbus's expeditions first reached the large island of Hispaniola—today the site of two nations: Haiti and the Dominican Republic. According to Frank M. Snowden:

By the NUMBERS

In the late 1400s and early 1500s, disease reduced Hispaniola's native population from some 1 million to about 15,000.

The native population of Hispaniola experienced a terrifying and unprecedented die-off. Between 1492 and 1520, the native population was reduced from 1 million to fifteen thousand. Agriculture, defense, and society itself disintegrated. . . . The [sickness] brought to the Americas by the Columbian [pandemic] therefore cleared Hispaniola for European colonization and Christian conversion almost before a shot was fired.[29]

Quarantining Africans with Smallpox

During the 1600s and beyond, African slaves appeared to be somewhat more resistant to smallpox than Native Americans had been. Nevertheless, White colonists found that the Africans still contracted the disease at rates that could cause more labor shortages. For that reason, it became common to quarantine sick Black slaves to keep them from infecting those who showed no disease symptoms. New York University's Elise A. Mitchell explains:

> If enslaved Africans appeared to be ill with smallpox or other contagious diseases, colonial officials sent them to the Isla de Cabras in Puerto Rico, Sullivan's Island in South Carolina, Tybee Creek in Georgia, . . . [and] countless other islets, coves, estuaries, and coastal locations. Slave traders would either disembark the enslaved or keep them aboard the ship for anywhere from two weeks to a few months, until the contagious disease ran its course. While many enslaved Africans who were quarantined for smallpox survived that virus, their lengthy quarantines aboard ships and on remote islands enabled [secondary] infections, parasites, and dysentery to spread.

> Because no one yet knew that unseen germs caused disease, European colonists sometimes caught smallpox from the slaves and spread the germs to others. In 1759, Mitchell says, infected British troops carried the disease into Charleston, South Carolina. "The outbreak severely disrupted the South Carolinian economy, and as panic spread, businesses closed and people fled. The public-health needs of the colony overwhelmed local physicians, who struggled to . . . treat the thousands of free and enslaved people who needed care."

Elise A. Mitchell, "The Shortages May Be Worse than the Disease," *The Atlantic*, March 11, 2020. www.theatlantic.com.

As awful as the demise of Hispaniola's original population was, its scope was small compared to that of the smallpox outbreak that struck central Mexico a few years later. Spanish soldiers led by military adventurer Hernán Cortés carried the deadly germs with them, likely unknowingly, when they invaded the lands of the Aztec and their neighbors beginning in 1519. The carnage was especially horrific during and after the Spanish siege of the Aztec capital, Tenochtitlán. A surviving native account recalls how the disease ran wild "for seventy days, striking everywhere in the city and killing a vast number of our people. Sores erupted on our faces, our breasts, our bellies. We were covered with agonizing sores from head to foot. The illness was so dreadful that no one could walk or move. The sick were so utterly helpless that they could only lie on their beds like corpses."[30]

In August 1521 Tenochtitlán fell to the Spaniards. The Aztec realm then simply ceased to exist, and the region soon became the Spanish colony of New Spain. Reflecting on how warlike foreigners had ravaged his homeland, a despairing Aztec poet wrote, "Broken spears lie in the roads," and "the houses are roofless now, and their walls are red with blood." He added, "Our inheritance, our city, is lost and dead. Know that with these disasters we have lost the Mexican nation."[31]

The Cocoliztli Outbreak

The 1520s witnessed the surviving Aztecs and other natives of the region reduced almost overnight into lowly servants of the triumphant Europeans. Dejected and miserable, the native peoples had reached what they assumed was their lowest ebb. They could not have foreseen that another onslaught of lethal disease would soon drive them even lower. Beginning in 1545 they once again began to die by the tens of thousands.

This time the major symptoms the victims displayed included high fever, dehydration, stomach and intestinal problems, yellowish skin, bleeding from the ears, hallucinations, and intense convulsions. Those who experienced all of these signs died within days. The locals called it *cocoliztli*, which in their language meant "pestilence."

> ### By the NUMBERS
>
> The 1545 *cocoliztli* outbreak in central Mexico killed an estimated 15 million people, amounting to about 45 percent of the native population.

The identity of the illness was largely a mystery to people of that era, including the Spaniards. Even most modern medical experts were unsure what it was until 2018, when researchers examined the DNA of actual victims of the sixteenth-century outbreak. "The evidence was tucked in the teeth of 29 skeletons unearthed from the ruins of an ancient [Mexican] city," science writer Angus Chen explains. The researchers "drilled into the skeletons' teeth and extracted DNA from that inner chamber. Once they had sequenced all the DNA, the team began comparing strands against a large database of modern bacterial pathogens."[32]

It turned out that the culprit was enteric fever, caused by salmonella—a common foodborne sickness. Experts think that, as in the case of the smallpox germs, European soldiers and settlers unwittingly brought the salmonella with them to the

This skull was found in the grave of an Aztec who died during the Spanish conquest of Mexico in the 1500s. The Spaniards transmitted smallpox germs to the Aztecs.

Americas. Once *cocoliztli* took hold and started to spread, Chen writes, "it swept through the region like a storm"[33] and claimed as many as 15 million lives.

Reshaping Human Futures

During the late sixteenth and early seventeenth centuries, small-pox, enteric fever, and other diseases continued to wipe out native populations, including those of the Caribbean islands. There, this trend steadily created a massive shortage of workers. In the earliest years of European colonization, White landowners and mine owners regularly found cheap labor among local populations. But over time disease outbreaks, along with brutal treatment, killed off a majority of the natives, threatening the profitability of plantations and mines.

To remedy the labor shortage, the owners of those industries turned to enslaving Black Africans. As Snowden tells it, after smallpox and other diseases helped White colonists take over the islands, "the near-disappearance of the native population drove the Europeans to find an alternative source of labor. The resulting turn to Africa was facilitated by the fact that the Africans were resistant to some of the same epidemic diseases that had destroyed the Native Americans. . . . In this way, disease was an important contributing factor in the development of slavery in the Americas."[34]

Thus, the enslavement of Africans—one of the darkest events in modern history—was in part a by-product of the overall Columbian pandemic. The centuries-long shipment of more than 12 million Africans to the Americas, scholars Nathan Nunn and Nancy Qian write, was triggered in large part by "the spread of Old World diseases to Native Americans, which resulted in extremely low [native] population densities in the New World."[35] Perhaps more than any other historical example, this demonstrates how disease germs can manipulate and reshape the fates, fortunes, and futures of entire human societies.

Chapter Four

Influenza Sweeps the World

The most destructive pandemic experienced in the United States during the twentieth century—that of the so-called Spanish flu—appeared in 1918, seemingly out of nowhere. Some idea of how serious the crisis was is captured in a letter to a friend penned in October of that year by a Native American nurse. She toiled nearly day and night on a Kansas Indian reservation. There, at the height of World War I, the government had set up a makeshift US Army camp. "As many as 90 people die every day here with the 'Flu,'" she wrote. "Orderlies carried the dead soldiers out on stretchers at the rate of two every three hours." She added with a touch of despair, "It is such a horrible thing, it is hard to believe, and yet such things happen [here] almost every day."[36]

Meanwhile, in the US capital, Washington, DC, local businessperson Bill Sardo's experiences and feelings mirrored those of most average American civilians. "From the moment I woke up in the morning to when I went to bed at night," he later recalled, "I felt a constant sense of fear. We wore gauze masks. We were afraid to kiss each other, to eat with each other, to have contact of any kind."[37]

The Spanish flu, a strain within a group of viruses collectively called influenza, struck in a series of broad waves. The first wave, which emerged in the spring of

1918, was fairly mild, but the second wave, which struck globally in August, was far more lethal. At first, tens of thousands of people died, and eventually the toll rose into the millions. The third wave came in early 1919 and claimed still more victims. Worldwide the flu killed at least 20 million souls, and some experts put the total closer to 50 million. (In comparison, roughly 10 million people died fighting in World War I.) In the United States the pandemic's victims numbered somewhere between 650,000 and 675,000.

A US army doctor and one of his nurses confer beside the bed of a victim of the Spanish flu in November 1918, during the great pandemic that killed tens of millions of people worldwide. As many as 675,000 Americans died of the disease.

Symptoms: From Mild to Severe

Not only did the outbreak's waves differ in strength, at times they featured somewhat different symptoms and levels of severity. Most of those who contracted the illness during the first wave experienced what today are viewed as typical flu symptoms—fever, chills, and fatigue. Of these victims, the vast majority recovered in several days and thereafter displayed immunity to the virus.

By contrast, during the flu's more deadly second wave, only a few people experienced mild symptoms. Far more numerous were those who had, in addition to fever and chills, more severe and painful reactions. Many were horrified to see their skin turn blue, and it was common for their lungs to fill with fluid, causing them to suffocate. For these individuals, death came speedily—in one to three days.

> **By the NUMBERS**
>
> Health experts estimate that the Spanish flu pandemic temporarily lowered life expectancy in the United States by twelve years.

Some unfortunates suffered from symptoms that were both gruesome and frightening. One hospital worker later recalled witnessing victims' bodies inexplicably filling with air. In such cases, he said, "air was trapped beneath their skin. As we rolled the dead up in sheets, their bodies crackled—an awful cracking noise which sounded like Rice Crispies when you pour milk over them."[38]

Communities Shuttered Out of Fear

Whatever symptoms the disease presented, one reality remained unchanged; namely, all attempts to halt or cure it proved futile. This is not surprising. No vaccine to protect people from the influenza virus had yet been found. Nor were there any antiviral drugs yet to help treat the contagion.

That left doctors and other health experts with only one viable approach—to do whatever they could to reduce the spread of the disease. Among those tactics were many of the ones employed

The Mask Slackers of 1918

During the 2020 COVID-19 pandemic, wearing face masks for safety reasons became controversial in some US cities and states. This was not the first time that people balked at wearing masks during a pandemic. An almost identical objection to mask wearing occurred during the devastating Spanish flu outbreak of 1918–1919. At the time, people who objected to donning masks derisively called them "dirt traps" or "muzzles." Similar to anti-mask sentiments in 2020, in 1918 those cloth shields stirred up political divisions. In the face of millions dying of Spanish flu, health officials urged everyone to wear a mask to help keep the virus from spreading—and most Americans complied.

But a vocal minority viewed mask wearing as a nefarious attempt to control the citizenry. Supporters of this view denounced mandatory mask-wearing regulations imposed in Seattle, Denver, San Francisco, and other cities. They also formed protest organizations, the biggest of which was the Anti-Mask League. Its members defied such rules and even refused to pay the five- and ten-dollar fines for violations; as a result, about one thousand of them were arrested in San Francisco in November 1918. Their jail times varied from eight hours to ten days. In meting out such sentences, one judge lectured the anti-maskers, whom most Americans called "slackers." Why did they not understand, he asked, that the masks were not meant to restrict people's freedom but rather to help keep them from getting sick?

in the more recent COVID-19 pandemic. One was quarantining, or isolating, people who were sick from the virus and those who had been exposed to infected people. Another was practicing good personal hygiene, including washing one's hands frequently and scrubbing often-touched surfaces with disinfectants. Health officials also urged people to limit the size of public gatherings, to stay several feet away from people one met in public (today called social distancing), and to wear a cloth mask over one's mouth and nose when in public.

On October 18, 1918, the Illustrated Current News *in New Haven, Connecticut, published a list of steps to take to avoid catching the Spanish flu, with a photograph of a Red Cross nurse wearing a mask. The list includes getting as much fresh air and sunshine as possible and wearing a protective mask.*

In addition, officials in many communities shut down most public places, including schools, libraries, churches, and theaters. Sardo later recalled that most people "had no school life, no church life, no community life. Fear tore people apart."[39] With schools closed, many parents turned to homeschooling their children, and the shuttered libraries stopped lending books. Meanwhile, numerous cities banned spitting in public—a common practice at the time. Related to that rule, members of New York City chapters of the Boys Scouts roamed the streets, and when they saw someone spit, they handed that person a card bearing the message "You are in violation of the Sanitary Code."[40]

From Public Bans to Super-Spreaders

In fact, in many US cities worry about contracting the virus was so prevalent that most people either avoided or altered deeply ingrained social and religious practices. In Chicago in late 1918, for example, local officials proclaimed:

There shall be no public funerals held in Chicago over any body dead from any disease whatsoever. No wakes or public gatherings of any kind shall be held in connection with these bodies. No one except adult relatives and friends, not to exceed ten persons in addition to the undertaker, undertaker's assistants, minister, and necessary drivers shall be permitted to attend any funeral.[41]

The effectiveness of curtailing funerals, banning large-scale public meetings, and wearing masks naturally depended on the willingness of most people to follow such rules. Many people chose not to follow them. A number of mayors and other local authorities viewed the pandemic as overhyped by the media and not as dangerous as it actually was. As a result, these individuals made decisions that proved tragic.

Philadelphia's response to the crisis was a sad case in point. One of the city's directors of public health, Wilmer Krusen, claimed

By the NUMBERS

The tiny American town of Brevig Mission, Alaska, lost 72 of its 80 residents to the Spanish flu.

that the mounting death toll was not caused by the Spanish flu but rather a different, less deadly form of flu. Therefore, he said, theaters and other public venues could remain open and a massive parade scheduled for September 28, 1918, to raise money for the war effort could be held as planned. Tens of thousands of people either marched in or watched the parade up close. Today this event would be called a "super-spreader" event.

Within two days of the parade, thousands of Philadelphians came down with Spanish flu, and eight days after that at least one thousand of them were dead. Over time, an estimated fifteen thousand Philadelphians who were involved in the parade or attended theaters and bars during the pandemic died. In contrast, in St. Louis, Missouri, where public facilities and events were banned early on, the overall death toll was only one-eighth that in Philadelphia.

The Nation Damaged in Many Ways

Complicating the pandemic considerably was that World War I had left sectors of the United States with a scarcity of doctors, nurses, and other health workers. Moreover, a fair number of those who *were* available ended up contracting the flu themselves, and some of them perished. Believed to be the first American nurse to die in the pandemic was North Carolina's Bessie C. Roper. According to an article on North Carolina nursing history, after Roper graduated from nursing school, she saw that a local college infirmary was overwhelmed with flu patients and volunteered to help. "Sadly she succumbed to the disease on October 22, 1918," the article states. "Her obituary appeared in many papers in the state lauding her selfless and noble sacrifice and likened her death to those of soldiers fighting on the battlefields of WWI. She was buried with military honors."[42]

By the NUMBERS

Some 62,000 American soldiers died of the Spanish flu, about 12,000 more than the number slain on the battlefields of World War I.

The loss of untold numbers of trained medical professionals during wartime was only one of many ways that the Spanish flu pandemic damaged the country. The national economy took an enormous hit, for instance. This happened in part thanks to tens of thousands of US businesses having to close their doors because so many employees had caught the virus.

At the same time, basic community services, among them mail delivery and garbage collection, slowed alarmingly. This was largely because the flu either killed or incapacitated many postal and trash collection workers. As a result, mail delivery slowed almost to a halt in some places, and garbage piled up into stinking

A Disease Detective Finds the 1918 Flu Virus

One reason the Spanish flu claimed so many victims was that scientists did not understand exactly how the virus worked and therefore were unable to fight and defeat it. Moreover, after the pandemic ended, experts who desired to study the virus lacked the knowledge and equipment required to isolate its DNA, or reproductive structure. Also, the virus itself had largely vanished, leaving few traces to study. Eventually, in 1951 a young Swedish microbiologist named Johan Hultin journeyed to the tiny town of Brevig Mission, Alaska, where the Spanish flu had killed most of the local population. He hoped but failed to find viable samples of the virus. However, he was more successful when he revisited the town in 1997. This time he discovered the body of a former female resident buried about 7 feet (2.1 m) deep in the icy permafrost. Hultin called her "Lucy." Fortunately, Lucy's lungs were perfectly preserved, and Hultin and some colleagues carefully studied them, allowing them to isolate the Spanish flu virus. They published their results in 1999, including the entire genetic code of the 1918 virus. It turned out that those germs originated in birds. Shortly before the 1918 outbreak, the study showed, the viruses made their way into some mammals, which then transmitted them to humans.

mounds on city streets. Similarly, some regions lacked enough physically healthy farmworkers to harvest the crops for a hungry nation, and millions of tons of vegetables and fruits rotted in fields and orchards.

The pandemic also negatively affected the war effort. In the space of less than a year, more US service members died from Spanish flu than were killed in battle. A staggering 40 percent of US Navy personnel came down with the virus, and the US Army was hit almost as hard, with 36 percent of its soldiers knocked out of action.

Meanwhile, damage to civilians, including young people, was sometimes no less harsh, often in a psychological sense. Seeing relatives and friends suffering and dying before their eyes, many young Americans learned firsthand that death is inevitable for all humans. In Brockton, Massachusetts, for example, student Francis Russell and his classmates stumbled upon the horrifying sight of grave diggers dumping corpses of flu victims into large unmarked graves. "In that bare instant," Russell later recalled, "I became aware of time. I knew then that life is not a perpetual present and . . . that for all my days and years to come I too must one day die. I pushed the relentless thought aside, knowing even as I did [that] I should never again be wholly free of it."[43]

The Estimated Death Toll Too Low?

By the summer of 1919, the flu pandemic came to an end as those who were infected either died or developed immunity. Other flu outbreaks struck the United States and other parts of the world later, including in 1957–1958 and 2009–2010. But none compared in scope and ferocity to the 1918–1919 pandemic. Indeed, "in sheer magnitude," J.N. Hays remarks, "the influenza pandemic of 1918–1919 stands as one of the great disease events of world history."[44]

Furthermore, the virus struck in many regions of the globe where accurate mortality figures were hard to come by. Historians are still studying and updating those figures, Hays continues, and it is a scary thought that "when historical evidence is more complete, the modern [upper] estimate of 50 million deaths may prove a serious understatement."[45]

Chapter Five

Polio: Shock Disease of the Modern Age

American surgeon Daly Walker has survived one pandemic only to experience another. The memories of that first pandemic are not happy ones. His experience with polio, one of the worst pandemics of the modern era, began in 1949. "For a couple days, I had suffered with a stuffy nose, feeling listless and sore all over," he remembers. Then, he says, while at bat in a local baseball game,

> a sharp pain shot up my neck and into my head. It frightened me. *What's this*? I thought. *What's wrong with me?* When I took a practice swing, the bat moved in slow motion as if it were a heavy broom. . . . My neck was so stiff and painful I had to turn my whole body to see [the coach]. As the ball came toward me, I closed my eyes and vomited. All my strength drained from my chest down my stomach and . . . I stumbled forward and fell into the dirt.[46]

Walker tried to stand but could not, and soon he could neither swallow nor eat. Tests performed at the county hospital confirmed that he had contracted poliomyelitis (then also called infantile paralysis), or polio for short. A viral disease, it most often strikes children younger than fourteen and can cause crippling paralysis.

The first known large-scale polio outbreak occurred in Sweden in 1881. That was followed by the disease's appearance in the US state of Vermont in 1894 and in New York State in 1907. As scary as these epidemics were, however, they were fairly localized and minor compared to a long-running outbreak that began in the United States in 1916. It reached its height of severity between 1949 and 1954.

A Disease Terrifying to Parents

The widespread modern fears of polio resulted from a combination of factors. First, it emerged suddenly, as if from nowhere, and rapidly became a major disease. Also, medical researchers were long unable to find a cure. Even more frightening was the way polio quickly paralyzed and often disfigured its victims, as well as claimed the lives of large numbers of them.

Public reactions to the crippling malady were highlighted by articles in popular publications. A 1935 issue of *Ladies' Home Journal*, for instance, stated that polio caused "mutilation worse than death."[47] That realization, coupled with the fact that the disease struck large numbers of children, made it perhaps the most terrifying modern pandemic for parents. Indeed, a prominent American doctor wrote in 1954, "There is literally no acute disease at the present day which causes so much apprehension and alarm in the patient and his relatives."[48] Similarly, that same year an essay in the widely read *Saturday Evening Post* said that polio "strikes more terror in the hearts of parents than the atom bomb."[49]

It may well have been that very factor—that polio was crippling and killing growing numbers of children—that inspired scientists and medical researchers of the early to mid-twentieth century to

By the NUMBERS

Reported cases of polio in the United States grew from 2,338 in 1920 to 57,879 in 1952.

Polio, which reached its height in the United States in the early 1950s, caused temporary or permanent paralysis. This 1954 photo shows two paralyzed women eating with the aid of specialized mechanical devices.

frantically seek a cure. The figures were indeed stark. In 1916 US cases topped twenty-eight thousand, a majority of them children, and of those roughly six thousand died. Thereafter, the number of cases continued to rise. In 1949 doctors diagnosed more than forty-two thousand cases of polio, again primarily children, and 1952 witnessed the emergence of an alarming fifty-eight thousand new victims.

Huge Fund-Raising Efforts

Motivation to develop a preventive vaccine was intense. Vaccines had been used in the past, yet never before had so much time and energy been given to such an effort. As J.N. Hays says, the obsession by American researchers to create a polio vaccine "made it the shock disease of the age, the one around which [the most] fear gathered."[50]

Ida's Story

Connecticut native Ida Curtis here summarizes how, despite contracting polio in her teens, she has managed to have a productive life.

I was eighteen years old in 1953 when I contracted polio. After the contagious stage, I was moved to Newington Home and Hospital for Crippled Children in Connecticut for rehabilitation. . . . After two years I had recovered the use of my arms and left the hospital in a wheelchair. In 1956 I married Jared, a fellow high school student with whom I corresponded during my hospital stay and . . . we soon had two children and I always tried hard to do my share of the work. Maintaining my independence and managing on my own when my husband travelled for his work was important to me. . . . Now, Jared and I have retired from our jobs and moved to a retirement community in an independent living apartment. There are lots of opportunities for social activities and recreation. I especially enjoy the swimming pool, where there is a lift that I can use to move in and out of the pool. . . . Aging with a disability brings a new challenge as I fear losing the ability to take care of my personal needs. . . . Using an electric scooter I'm able to do most of the grocery shopping. I especially enjoy this task as it means exploring the city, and I will continue doing it as long as possible.

Ida Curtis, "What Having a Disability Taught Me," Polio Place. www.polioplace.org.

It became clear that such a massive effort by thousands of scientists and doctors in the United States alone would require enormous amounts of money to launch and maintain. Huge fundraising drives were therefore necessary. For that reason, Hays explains, polio became the modern disease "against which a new scale of private philanthropy [charity efforts] was mobilized in the search for . . . preventative vaccines."[51]

The first large-scale movement to raise money for polio re-search kicked off not long after Franklin D. Roosevelt first won election as US president in 1932. Roosevelt had been stricken with polio eleven years before. "When I swung out of bed," he later remembered, "my left leg lagged. But I managed to move about to shave. I tried to persuade myself that the trouble with my leg was muscular . . . but presently, it refused to work, and then the other [leg became paralyzed]."[52]

Roosevelt never recovered physically. Yet faced with a seri-ous, permanent disability, he displayed tremendous courage and determination—both of which helped him win election as New York governor and eventually as US president. His personal battle against polio impressed Americans and stirred them to give mon-ey each year to help fund the search for a polio vaccine. Because at first millions of citizens sent dimes to the charity overseeing the fund-raising effort, it soon became known as the March of Dimes.

Initial Difficulties and Failures

In this way, during the 1930s and 1940s polio research was fund-ed to the tune of tens of millions of dollars, then an unprecedented amount collected to fight any disease. The scientists involved in the effort tried hard to make every dollar count. But as is often the case in modern scientific research, many of the approaches they employed in finding a vaccine initially led them down blind alleys.

A vaccine is a safely altered form of a disease-causing mi-crobe that stimulates the body to build up immunity to that illness. The original goal for a polio vaccine was to try to weaken the polio virus. Researchers doused the germs with chemicals they thought would make the disease-causing agents impotent. The hope was that the still living virus would trigger immunity in those vaccinated but would be too weak to make them sick. However, when the first two experimental vaccines were each injected into eleven thousand volunteers in 1935, some of those individuals came down with polio and died. Subsequent studies showed that the chemicals used to weaken the germs had not affected all of them. Other polio vaccines developed in the late 1930s and early 1940s were also unsuccessful.

An important lesson that researchers learned from these failures has affected the course of vaccine research ever since. Namely, one reason that the initial polio vaccines produced the most feared outcome—more illness or death—was that the scientists tasked with developing them were under enormous pressure to work fast. This factor led some of them to take shortcuts, which in turn increased the likelihood of making mistakes.

Another factor that led to early failures was that researchers at the time lacked a full understanding of the disease. For instance, their initial assumption that a single virus caused polio turned out to be incorrect. The reality is that more than one hundred strains of polio virus exist, and a vaccine that works with one strain is frequently useless against others.

Enter Jonas Salk

In the late 1940s, however, as the number of US cases of polio continued to grow each year, the pressure to find a workable vaccine increased. First, in 1948 a brilliant young researcher named Jonas Salk joined the fight against the disease. He painstakingly studied and carefully classified many polio virus strains, which provided a major boost to the overall antipolio effort.

This and other advances inspired Salk to work harder than ever. Well funded by various organizations and donors, in 1951 he hired more than fifty experts in biology, chemistry, and immunology. In the two years that followed, they worked long hours in the lab, with Salk himself logging eighteen hours a day, seven days a week. He later compared this pivotal period of research to the invention of a new kind of cake. One begins, he said, "with an idea and certain ingredients, and then experiments, a little more of this, a little less of that, and keeps changing things."[53]

By the NUMBERS

Jonas Salk oversaw the 1954 clinical trial in which about 2 million children were vaccinated against polio.

Medical researchers around the globe desperately tried to create a vaccine to prevent polio. The first major success was that of Dr. Jonas Salk in 1954. In this photo he is seen ten years later personally administering his vaccine to a young patient.

The recipe, so to speak, for Salk's cake ended up using three major polio virus strains. Instead of using chemicals to weaken the germs, he out-and-out killed them with a powerful chemical. Repeated experiments with monkeys in 1953 indicated that a virus killed in that manner still produced an immune response in those animals. Next, Salk bravely vaccinated himself and, with their permission, the members of his family. A few months later, in April 1954, he oversaw the vaccination of some 1.8 million children aged six to nine.

A Dream Becomes Reality

Salk's vaccine was a resounding success. It proved to be both effective and safe. In April 1955 the US secretary of health, education, and welfare, Oveta C. Hobby, approved the vaccine for large-scale manufacture and distribution. "It's a wonderful day for the whole world," she remarked. "It's a history-making day."[54]

People across the United States and around the world received the vaccine, and by 1961 the yearly number of new US cases of polio dropped below five hundred. Salk was hailed as a hero, as was a colleague, Albert B. Sabin of the University of Cincinnati College of Medicine. Sabin developed a second safe and effective polio vaccine that produced an even stronger immune response than Salk's. With the combined efforts of the two vaccines, polio almost disappeared in the United States, Canada, Europe, and Asia by 1969. This outcome had been the hope of thousands of scientists decades before, and now that the vaccines had done their work, a researcher pointed out what Salk himself had said about hope. It "lies in dreams," he suggested, "in imagination, and in the courage of those who dare to make dreams into reality."[55]

Standing on the shoulders of many other researchers, Salk had indeed turned a distant dream into reality. The dramatic defeat of polio was one of the great triumphs of modern science. The disease was not totally eradicated. It still crops up here and there, mainly in the only three countries that do not routinely vaccinate children—Pakistan, Afghanistan, and Nigeria. But it is no longer the widespread crippler and killer it once was, because medical science, aided by the government and the general citizenry, applied the money, time, ingenuity, and sheer tenacity required to tame it. The victory over polio, Frank M. Snowden points out, was a lesson for humanity for the ages. It "clearly demonstrates," he declares, "that the eradication of an epidemic disease requires adequate tools, extensive funding, careful organization, sustained effort, and good fortune."[56]

Chapter Six

The Ongoing Search for an HIV/AIDS Cure

In 2004 a young woman who calls herself Aimee dis-covered that she had become a victim of one of the most frightening diseases to emerge in the twentieth century. She later recalled:

> I had a strange bruise-like spot on my left breast that continued to get bigger and bigger. Soon, it covered my entire breast. I went to 7 differ-ent doctors and no one knew what it was. . . . [Finally a doctor told] me that it was something called Kaposi's Sarcoma. Found only in end-stage AIDS patients. . . . I remember thinking that it was a nightmare and I would soon wake up. My family sat around and mourned for me. We all thought I was dead.[57]

As the months went on, Aimee endured several seemingly unrelated physical ailments, including skin rashes and severe hair loss. This was not unusual, she learned. Her doctor explained that AIDS (acquired im-munodeficiency syndrome) damages the immune sys-tem, leaving the infected person vulnerable to contract-ing a wide range of illnesses. He also told her that AIDS is caused by a virus called HIV (human immunodeficiency virus). HIV and AIDS are technically not the same thing, but they are related. Some people infected with HIV never develop AIDS, which is a late-stage result of HIV infection that emerges only when the virus has seriously compromised the immune system. Because this leaves victims open to a wide range of diseases, the symptoms of AIDS can vary considerably from person to person.

Medical Authorities Taken by Surprise

The great HIV/AIDS pandemic, which in some parts of the world is ongoing, began when the virus suddenly and mysteriously appeared in May 1981. Five cases of young men with impaired immune systems were reported by medical authorities in New York City, and in the months that followed, many more cases emerged in other cities, as well as other countries. It soon became clear to the medical community that most of the infected people had been ill for some time. They had caught the disease, whatever it was, months or years before and were only now displaying advanced symptoms.

The question was: What was causing these attacks on the immune system? It was not until two years later that a team of American medical researchers led by Robert C. Gallo isolated the culprit. It was a virus that later become known as HIV.

The virus spread with amazing rapidity during the 1980s and 1990s. By 1993 nearly 3 million cases had been confirmed worldwide. Only two years later the Centers for Disease Control and Prevention (CDC) announced that the disease had become the leading cause of death for Americans aged twenty-five to forty-four. In 1994, for example, the CDC reported 41,900 US AIDS deaths, 72 percent of which were among people aged twenty-five to forty-four. Moreover, several other nations reported similar figures.

These disturbing facts took the global medical community largely by surprise. They also made many doctors and other medical experts

By the NUMBERS

Almost 33 million people worldwide have died of AIDS since 1981.

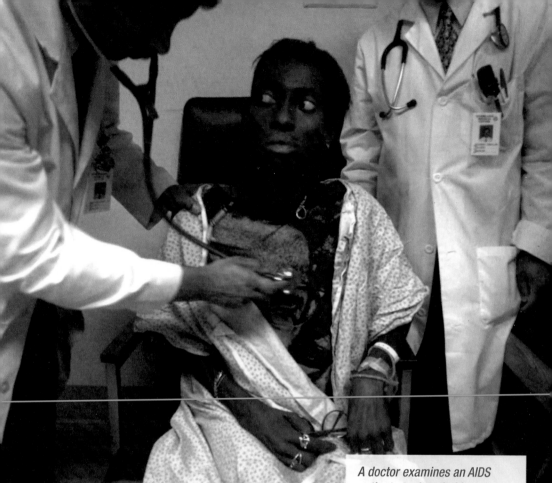

A doctor examines an AIDS patient at a hospital in November 1997. Over time, scientists learned that AIDS can be contracted by people of any age, any gender, any sexual orientation, and all walks of life.

rethink their view of the possible danger of large disease outbreaks in modern society. Indeed, as the pandemic swept around the globe, leaving millions dead in its wake, it became a sort of wake-up call to developed countries with advanced medical systems, notably the United States, United Kingdom, France, Germany, Canada, and Australia. J.N Hays points out that the sudden arrival of HIV/AIDS

marked the end of an era. In the years after World War II, Americans [and Europeans] had become convinced that violent and uncontrollable epidemics were things of the past. That conviction stemmed in part from the re-markable [reduction of] such diseases as tuberculosis and syphilis, and in part from the development of successful preventative vaccines. The most dramatic vaccine [stories had been those] of polio in the 1950s [and] the eradication of smallpox from the human population by 1977. Biomedical science had seemed to have conquered the world of epidemic disease. AIDS challenged and in many ways overthrew that optimism.[58]

A vaccine for HIV/AIDS has been elusive for a variety of reasons. Because HIV directly targets the body's immune system itself, the immune system does not produce the immune response that a vaccine seeks to create in order to fight off the

How HIV Entered the Human Population

Scientists believe HIV originated in apes, especially chimpanzees and gorillas, and somehow crossed the interspecies barrier into humans. Only after that did sexual contact become the primary means of transmission. According to medical researcher Peter C. Doherty:

> The idea that is most favored for the crossover of HIV strains into our species is that these viruses "jumped" during the harvesting of "bush meat." As human population sizes have increased and starvation has become an ever-present threat, the practice of killing wild-living primates (bush meat) for human food is thought to have become much more prevalent. An obvious possibility is that someone could have cut their hand and contracted one or other HIV variant as a consequence of blood contaminating an open wound while butchering a chimp [or] a gorilla. . . . Once that happened, all the epidemiological data we have is consistent with the perception that sexual transmission has been, and is, the main mechanism of HIV spread.

Peter C. Doherty, *Pandemics: What Everyone Needs to Know.* New York: Oxford University Press, 2013, p. 130.

disease. "The very concept underlying vaccination," say medical researchers Anna Aldovini and Richard A. Young, "is not applicable for an infection from which there is no evidence that a person can recover." Indeed, "if the immune system cannot mount an effective response, scientists may not be able to design an AIDS vaccine."[59]

Acting Out of Ignorance and Fear

As late as 2020 no effective HIV vaccine yet existed. One reason for this, some experts say, is fear—which translated to less money for such research. In the early 1980s, as the disease emerged into public view, the vast majority of the disease's victims were gay males or drug addicts (who often shared drug needles). This created a misconception that members of those groups were the only people who could or did contract the ailment. In turn, that misguided belief generated a great deal of cruel and hateful treatment of the victims. As Frank M. Snowden tells it:

> The onset of a "gay plague" revived the oldest of all interpretations of epidemic diseases—that they are the "wages of sin" meted out by a wrathful god. Recalling biblical [passages] . . . some conservative religious leaders took the lead in propounding this view. Jerry Falwell, founder of the Moral Majority, gained instant notoriety by famously declaring that AIDS was God's punishment not just for homosexuals, but for a society that tolerated homosexuals.[60]

Contracting HIV had nothing to do with morality. Instead, the initial victims tended to unwisely put themselves at a higher risk of infection by either practicing unprotected sex or using contaminated needles. As a result, HIV quite naturally attacked those individuals first and spread quickly among them. Yet as society would soon discover, anyone could acquire the disease. This became apparent as time went on; HIV infected both males and females, gay and straight, and people from every race, religion, and socioeconomic level.

Still, recognition of the fact that HIV/AIDS did not discriminate among its human victims was slow to register within the general public. The result was that the social stigma remained in effect for several years and caused acts of discrimination that today are seen as ignorant and shameful. In 1983, for example, a New York physician who offered AIDS victims help was threatened with eviction from the building housing his offices. Similarly, a large number of schools across the nation barred children infected with HIV from attending. This was in spite of doctors' assurances that the virus spread *only* through entering one's bloodstream and was therefore not contagious in the same manner as airborne and waterborne diseases.

Lawmakers in Washington, DC, also discriminated out of ignorance and fear. In 1987 the federal government enacted a travel ban on visitors and immigrants with HIV despite the extremely low likelihood of their transmitting the disease. In addition, federal officials at first refused to fund needle exchange programs, which scientists explained would effectively reduce HIV transmission. As a result, some experts estimate, close to ten thousand people acquired HIV who may not have if they had had access to clean needles.

Improving Their Quality of Life

Societal attitudes toward HIV/AIDS eventually began to change. This occurred in part because a number of well-known people admitted that they had contracted the virus. The first of these celebrities to come forward was actor Rock Hudson. When he died of AIDS in 1985, he left $250,000 to set up an AIDS foundation. Rock idol Freddie Mercury of the band Queen also died

Popular singer Freddie Mercury, of the rock group Queen, performs in a concert in Sydney, Australia, in 1985. In 1991, Mercury died of AIDS, an event that made headlines around the globe and brought much attention to the HIV/AIDS crisis.

from AIDS-related conditions in 1991. That same year basketball superstar Earvin "Magic" Johnson made headlines when he admitted that he had contracted HIV.

These and other celebrities brought attention to the HIV/AIDS pandemic, which killed almost 700,000 people worldwide in 2019 and close to 33 million since 1981. As a result, each year more and more organizations and individuals make contributions to efforts to find an HIV vaccine. Although as late as 2020 that goal was still unfulfilled, hundreds of scientists around the globe remained committed to achieving it. In the meantime, their efforts did result in a number of treatments that have significantly improved the lives of those infected with HIV. Some consist of drugs that slow the virus's invasion of healthy cells. Other medications—called inhibitors—make it much harder for the HIV virus to copy itself after it invades the cells. Another drug in use today reduces the risk of catching HIV from sexual activity by more than 90 percent.

Young Stan's Ordeal

The HIV/AIDS pandemic has affected and continues to affect people of all genders, all ages, all nations, and every socioeconomic group. One American sufferer, who when interviewed about his ordeal called himself Stan, was only thirteen when he was infected with HIV in 1989. During the summer of that year, he fell in love with a young woman several years older than he was, and they ended up having sexual relations. In August Stan noticed some small red spots on his skin. He also found it odd that he seemed to be unusually tired much of the time. That fall he entered high school, and in preparation for joining the swimming team he underwent a routine physical exam. Not long afterward he learned that the exam revealed that he had been infected with HIV. He later recalled:

> At first we thought there must have been a mistake and that the test must have been switched. So I took another test and that one was positive, too. I told the woman I'd been dating, . . . and within 24 hours she was gone. I never heard from her again. I started getting really angry that at 14, I had this life-threatening disease. I had dreams about going to college, making money. But how could I plan for college when I didn't know if I was going to live another year?

Quoted in HealthyPlace, "Teens Living with AIDS: Three People's Stories," August 22, 2014. www.healthyplace.com.

Meanwhile, optimism for an actual cure came in 2019. Doctors in England announced that a man they called the "London patient" had become totally HIV-free after undergoing bone marrow replacement. A year later that individual, Adam Castillejo, went public, saying, "I want to be an ambassador of hope."[61] Soon afterward, Anton Pozniak, president of the International AIDS Society, marked that momentous occasion, saying that Castillejo's experience reaffirms the long-held hope of millions of sufferers worldwide—the "belief that there exists a proof of concept that HIV is curable."[62]

Chapter Seven

The Latest Global Pandemic: COVID-19

"Doctors and nurses hurry through the surgical ICU hallway, bathed in yellow light," *Washington Post* medical reporter Lenny Bernstein wrote in early April 2020. "There is no time for wasted motion. They wear white lab coats or blue gowns, with hair coverings, gloves, face masks and goggles, their shoes protected by disposable booties. . . . Without looking, they poke at ubiquitous hand-sanitizer dispensers and rub their hands as they speed by."[63]

Bernstein frantically tried to keep up with the dedicated doctors and nurses at Maimonides Medical Center in Brooklyn, New York. Like hundreds of other US hospitals, it was besieged by an onslaught of cases of the debilitating respiratory disease COVID-19. During Bernstein's visit, fully 80 percent of Maimonides's six hundred adult patients were suffering from COVID-19, a percentage destined to rise even higher in the following weeks.

The chaotic, unprecedented conditions inside the hospital in some ways mirrored what was happening outside its walls. There, Bernstein pointed out, COVID-19 was sweeping the globe, including the United States, and the virus had "disrupted everything about the way people live." In a growing number of cities, shops and businesses had shut down, and untold millions of people had begun sheltering in their homes in hopes of avoiding the spreading contagion. Inside the hospitals, meanwhile, Bernstein continued, the disease had "mercilessly altered the way [people] convalesce and die. Like every hospital in New York state, Maimonides has banned almost all visitors until the final hours before death, when a single family member is allowed to witness the passing."[64]

Part of what made the outbreak disruptive and scary was the suddenness of the appearance of a new coronavirus and the disease that resulted from it. It had quietly and ominously emerged in late December 2019 in Wuhan, China, and in early January 2020 the Chinese National Health Commission had alerted the World Health Organization (WHO). Following existing procedure, authorities at WHO then relayed a warning to health services worldwide. Shortly afterward, on February 11, the International Committee on Taxonomy of Viruses (the group of scientists tasked with naming viral diseases) gave the disease the official name of COVID-19 (for *coronavirus disease 2019*).

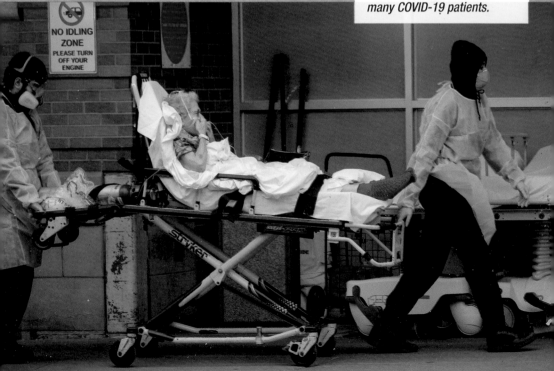

A woman struggling to breathe arrives at the emergency room at Maimonides Medical Center, in Brooklyn, on April 14, 2020. She was one of New York's many COVID-19 patients.

Why the Virus Spread So Rapidly

By the time the disease received its name, about ten thousand people, mostly in China, had displayed symptoms. Realizing WHO officials' worst fears, that figure rapidly increased. By mid-March 2020, COVID-19 had infected a quarter of a million people worldwide, becoming a full-fledged global pandemic. As awful as that figure seemed at the time, it proved a mere foreshadowing of the horrors to come. By mid-September 2020, the virus had infected some 30.2 million people globally and killed almost 1 million.

Shocked by these figures, many people asked how and why the disease had spread so far and so fast. Scientists and health care experts responded that there were multiple reasons. One, they explained, is that in most countries, even in wealthier ones like the United States and United Kingdom, not enough money had been invested in recent years in public health, decent low-cost housing, and sanitation. That had led to increasingly crowded living conditions in cities around the globe, making them breeding grounds for disease germs.

By the **NUMBERS**

As of September 9, 2020, the United States had 6.5 million coronavirus infections and nearly 200,000 COVID-19 deaths, more than any other nation.

Another factor, the experts pointed out, was a huge expansion of global connectedness, with travel and trade bringing people of nearly all nations into contact with one another. "Once public health fails and contagion appears anywhere," science writer Debora MacKenzie writes, "it goes everywhere. We know so much about beating disease, yet fragmented governing structures, lack of global accountability, and persistent poverty in so many places ensure that those failures happen and disease propagates."[65]

The Misinformation Factor

Another major factor that allowed the virus to spread so far and so quickly took the form of widespread confusion, misinformation, and conspiracy theories. Dr. Seema Yasmin, director of the Stanford Health Communication Initiative, and Dr. Craig Spencer of New York's Columbia University Medical

Center studied and reported on this growing and disturbing phenomenon. In the midst of "the worst pandemic of our lifetime," they reported in late August 2020, "the virus continues to spread alongside medical myths and health hoaxes. False news is not a new phenomenon, but it has been amplified by social media. . . . Websites spreading health hoaxes on Facebook peaked at an estimated 460 million views on the platform in April 2020 . . . just as the virus was spreading around the world and overwhelming hospitals."[66]

Typical of the false claims made about COVID and the pandemic in 2020 was that it was purposely manufactured in a Chinese lab and unleashed on an unsuspecting world. This idea continued to circulate widely around the world despite medical studies of the virus's structure that prove it untrue.

In some countries, government officials have contributed to the steady stream of misinformation. For instance, Brazil's president, Jair Bolsonaro, has described COVID-19 as little more than a mild flu. Brazil is second only to the United States in COVID-19 deaths. US president Donald Trump has also been widely criticized by scientists and medical authorities for making false or misleading statements about the disease. For example, as COVID-19 deaths in the United States approached 200,000 (and coronavirus infections reached into the millions), Trump falsely proclaimed at a September 21, 2020, Ohio rally that "it affects virtually nobody."[67] An August 2020 report in the Atlantic magazine charged, "Trump has repeatedly downplayed the significance of COVID-19" and the pandemic. "From calling criticism of his handling of the virus a 'hoax,' to comparing the coronavirus to the common flu . . . Trump has used his public statements to send mixed messages and sow doubt about the outbreak's seriousness."[68]

The Failure of US Contact Tracing

When COVID-19 became a global pandemic in early 2020, health authorities around the world put into place measures designed to slow and if possible halt the spread of the disease. Among them were sheltering in place at home, social distancing, washing one's hands regularly, and wearing face masks in public. Still another was contact tracing, designed to track down and if necessary quarantine any and all people with whom an infected person has recently had close contact. Olga Khazan, a staff writer for *Atlantic* magazine, provides the following concise description of how contact tracing is meant to work:

> Let's say Aunt Sally tests positive for COVID-19. A tracer working for the local public-health department calls her and asks for her contacts—anyone she's spent more than 15 minutes with recently—and asks her to self-isolate. Then the tracer calls those "close contacts" of Aunt Sally's, and asks *them* to self-isolate too. The tracer doesn't tell Aunt Sally's contacts that she is the person who tested positive, only that someone they were in contact with did.

By September 2020 it was clear that contact tracing was not working well in the United States. One reason for that, Khazan explains, is the high number of COVID cases in the country. The bigger the number of infected people, the more tracers required, and some cities could not afford to hire so many. Also, some Americans distrust the federal government and as a result refused to help with contact tracing.

Olga Khazan, "The Most American COVID-19 Failure Yet," *The Atlantic*, August 31, 2020. www.theatlantic.com.

Safety Measures and a Lopsided Death Toll

Still another factor that helped the virus spread far and wide was that certain groups in society were unable—or, in some instances, unwilling—to enact basic safety protocols, or measures. With no vaccine available, the best that people around the globe could do was to practice such measures. These included sheltering at home when possible, washing one's hands frequently, and social distancing and wearing masks when in public.

As had occurred during the 1918 Spanish flu pandemic, some people have resisted sheltering at home and wearing masks. The most common complaint, heard especially in the United States, is that these measures impinge on personal liberty. This view was evident in August 2020 when 400,000 motorcycle enthusiasts gathered in South Dakota for the annual Sturgis Motorcycle Rally. Few of the attendees wore masks or practiced social distancing—and the result was several hundred new cases of COVID-19. In general, however, people worldwide have attempted to follow most or all of the protocols, even if somewhat reluctantly.

Those who were unable to enact such health guidelines— because of their work, living situations, or lack of access to health care—suffered more than others, according to studies based on data from Johns Hopkins University and other reputable sources. These studies showed a decidedly lopsided pattern in the ongoing pandemic's death toll. In the United States, for instance, a disproportionate number of Black and Hispanic citizens died from the virus, in some cities at twice or more the rate of White citizens. Such differences are too big to be mere random chance, medical experts say. Rather, members of those groups are more likely to be poor and to have less access to adequate health care. Also, as science writer Leslie Nemo explains in an article for *Discover* magazine:

> Black and Hispanic people are more likely to work in frontline jobs, such as child care or grocery store positions, that cannot be done from home. . . . [Also] while the Black population makes up 12 percent of the overall workforce, 26 percent of public transit employees are Black. Hispanics make up 17 percent of the workforce, but 40 percent of all building custodial work. To add one more layer in major cities, such as New York, these populations face extra exposure while commuting to and from work on public transit.[69]

Racing to Find a Vaccine

From the start of the COVID-19 pandemic, experts emphasized that the safety protocols that some people were able to practice regularly and others less frequently constituted a temporary measure that a vaccine would eventually replace. Indeed, as early as February 2020 labs in more than a dozen countries launched programs to find a vaccine to fight the disease. It was clear to medical experts everywhere that any success would not be achieved quickly. The usual process of developing a vaccine is complex and time consuming. After months or years of fashioning a potential vaccine, researchers typically test it on animals first. Assuming it proves effective and safe, three phases of human trials generally follow. The first determines whether the vaccine is safe for small groups of people; in the second phase, researchers establish the safest and most effective doses; and the third phase finds out whether the vaccine is safe to use on the general population. If the vaccine passes all three phases, which normally takes years, it is licensed and then manufactured and distributed on a large scale.

By the NUMBERS

By September 9, 2020, US airports had screened some 684,000 international passengers to see whether they displayed any symptoms of COVID-19.

By September 2020 more than one hundred potential vaccines for COVID-19 were under development worldwide. Hoping to speed up the regular process, makers of ten of those possible remedies skipped phase one and went straight to human trials. One was the National Institutes of Health, which began conducting tests on thirty thousand human subjects in the late summer of 2020. The first vaccine candidate tested was one developed at the biotechnology company Moderna, based in Cambridge, Massachusetts.

Even if one of the ten most promising vaccines proves effective and safe, it must be stressed that COVID-19 will not simply go away. Like influenza, it may well remain a threat for generations to

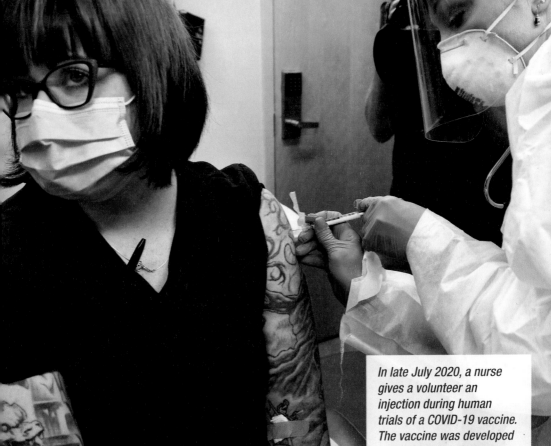

In late July 2020, a nurse gives a volunteer an injection during human trials of a COVID-19 vaccine. The vaccine was developed by the National Institutes of Health and a private research company, Moderna.

come and continue to plague those who are not vaccinated for it. Also, the way that the virus appeared unexpectedly and killed almost 1 million people in only a few months serves stark notice to humanity that nature harbors a seemingly endless reservoir of dangerous germs. As science writer Richard Conniff aptly puts it:

> We have entered a frightening new world. Or maybe we are returning to the old world of our disease-plagued ancestors. The one great lesson we should take away from history is this: When the current pandemic ultimately subsides, we cannot afford to forget that this happened. We cannot just move on. Somewhere on the planet, the next great pandemic, the next destroying angel, is already taking wing.[70]

Source Notes

Introduction: Learning the Lessons of Past Pandemics

1. Richard Conniff, "How Pandemics Have Changed Us," *National Geographic*, August, 2020, p. 47.
2. Peter C. Doherty, *Pandemics: What Everyone Needs to Know*. New York: Oxford University Press, 2013, p. 42.
3. Conniff, "How Pandemics Have Changed Us," p. 58.
4. Quoted in Joan E. Knight, "The Social Impact of the Influenza Pandemic of 1918–1919," PhD dissertation, University of Nottingham, 2015, p. 2.
5. Quoted in Debora MacKenzie, *COVID-19: The Pandemic That Never Should Have Happened*. New York: Hachette, 2020, p. 242.

Chapter One: Pandemic Diseases in the Ancient Era

6. William H. McNeill, *Plagues and Peoples*. New York: Random House, 1998, p. 36.
7. McNeill, *Plagues and Peoples*, pp. 60–61.
8. Quoted in Trevor Bryce, *Life and Society in the Hittite World*. New York: Oxford University Press, 2002, p. 78.
9. Quoted in McNeill, *Plagues and Peoples*, p. 96.
10. Deuteronomy 22:28, Revised Standard Version.
11. Thucydides, *The Peloponnesian War*, trans. Rex Warner. New York: Penguin, 1972, p. 152.
12. Quoted in R.J. Littman and M.L. Littman, "Galen and the Antonine Plague," *American Journal of Philology*, Autumn 1973, p. 246.

13. Procopius, *History of the Wars*, vol. 1, trans. H.B. Dewing. Cambridge, MA: Harvard University Press, 1914, pp. 59, 61.
14. J.N. Hays, *Epidemics and Pandemics: Their Impacts on Human History*. Santa Barbara, CA: ABC-CLIO, 2005, p. 24.

Chapter Two: The Black Death Devastates Europe

15. Quoted in George Deaux, *The Black Death 1347*. New York: Weybright and Talley, 1969, pp. 93–94.
16. Giovanni Boccaccio, *The Decameron*, trans. Mark Musa and Peter Bondanella. New York: Norton, 1982, pp. 10–11.
17. Frank M. Snowden, *Epidemics and Society: From the Black Death to the Present*. New Haven, CT: Yale University Press, 2019, p. 29.
18. Quoted in Medieval Source Book, "Jean Froissart: On the Jacquerie, 1358," January 2, 2020. www.fordham.edu.
19. Quoted in Susan Scott and Christopher J. Duncan, *Return of the Black Death: The World's Greatest Serial Killer*. Chichester, UK: Wiley, 2004, pp. 14–15.
20. Quoted in Rosemary Horrox, ed., *The Black Death*. Manchester, UK: Manchester University Press, 1994, p. 126.
21. Boccaccio, *The Decameron*, p. 6.
22. Philip Ziegler, *The Black Death*. New York: Harper and Row, 1969, p. 279.
23. Quoted in Horrox, *The Black Death*, pp. 160–61.
24. Ziegler, *The Black Death*, p. 279.

Chapter Three: Conquest and Disease: The Columbian Plagues

25. Hays, *Epidemics and Pandemics*, p. 79.
26. McNeill, *Plagues and Peoples*, pp. 223–24.
27. Francisco Hernández Arana Xajilá, *The Annals of the Cakchiquels*, trans. Adrian Recinos et al. Norman: University of Oklahoma Press, 1953, p. 58.
28. McNeill, *Plagues and Peoples*, pp. 20–21.

29. Snowden, *Epidemics and Society*, pp. 102–103.
30. Quoted in Miguel León-Portilla, ed., *The Broken Spears: The Aztec Account of the Conquest of Mexico*. Boston: Beacon, 1992, pp. 92–93.
31. Quoted in León-Portilla, *The Broken Spears*, pp. 137–39.
32. Angus Chen, "One of History's Worst Epidemics May Have Been Caused by a Common Microbe," *Science*, January 16, 2018. www.sciencemag.org.
33. Chen, "One of History's Worst Epidemics May Have Been Caused by a Common Microbe."
34. Snowden, *Epidemics and Society*, p. 103.
35. Nathan Nunn and Nancy Qian, "The Columbian Exchange: A History of Disease, Food, and Ideas," *Journal of Economic Perspectives*, Spring 2010, p. 181.

Chapter Four: Influenza Sweeps the World

36. Quoted in National Archives, "Letter from Nurse to Her Friend at the Haskell Indian Nations University, Kansas, October 17, 1918." www.archives.gov.
37. Quoted in Lynette Iezzoni, *Influenza 1918: The Worst Epidemic of American History*. New York: Open Library, 1999, p. 154.
38. Quoted in Iezzoni, *Influenza 1918*, p. 120.
39. Quoted in Iezzoni, *Influenza 1918*, p. 154.
40. Quoted in Susan Dominus, "In 1918 Flu Outbreak, a Cool Head Prevailed," *New York Times*, May 1, 2009. www.nytimes.com.
41. Quoted in Catherine Arnold, *Pandemic 1918*. New York: St. Martin's, 2018, p. 135.
42. "NC Nurses Who Died 'on Duty' During the Influenza Epidemic From 1918–1920," North Carolina Nursing History, Appalachian State University, 2018. https://nursinghistory.appstate.edu.
43. Quoted in Iezzoni, *Influenza 1918*, p. 81.
44. Hays, *Epidemics and Pandemics*, p. 385.
45. Hays, *Epidemics and Pandemics*, p. 386.

Chapter Five: Polio: Shock Disease of the Modern Age

46. Daly Walker, "A Tale of Two Viruses," *Saturday Evening Post*, June 8, 2020. www.saturdayeveningpost.com.
47. Paul De Kruif, "Polio Must Go," *Ladies' Home Journal*, July 1, 1935, p. 22.
48. Quoted in Harold Faber and Doris Faber, *American Heroes of the 20th Century*. New York: Random House, 1967, p. 71.
49. Quoted in Faber and Faber, *American Heroes of the 20th Century*, p. 72.
50. Hays, *Epidemics and Pandemics*, p. 377.
51. Hays, *Epidemics and Pandemics*, p. 377.
52. Quoted in Hugh G. Ghallager, *FDR's Splendid Deception: The Moving Story of Roosevelt's Massive Disability and the Intense Efforts to Conceal It from the Public*. New York: Dodd, Mead, 1985, p. 23.
53. Quoted in Faber and Faber, *American Heroes of the 20th Century*, p. 93.
54. Quoted in Faber and Faber, *American Heroes of the 20th Century*, p. 98.
55. Quoted in Karen Berger, "The Virus Research of Jonas Salk Led to Polio Vaccine," *Pharmacy Times*, February 28, 2019. www.pharmacytimes.com.
56. Snowden, *Epidemics and Society*, p. 407.

Chapter Six: The Ongoing Search for an HIV/AIDS Cure

57. Quoted in HealthyPlace, "AIDS True Stories," 2020. www.healthyplace.com.
58. Hays, *Epidemics and Pandemics*, p. 429.
59. Anna Aldovini and Richard A. Young, "The New Vaccines," *Technology Review*, January 1992, p. 27.
60. Snowden, *Epidemics and Society*, p. 436.
61. Quoted in Trenton Straube, "Meet the 2nd Person Cured of HIV, a.k.a. the 'London Patient,'" *POZ*, March 9, 2020. www.poz.com.

62. Quoted in Sarah Boseley, "Tests on London Patient Offer Hope of HIV 'Cure,'" *The Guardian* (Manchester, UK), March 5, 2019. www.theguardian.com.

Chapter Seven: The Latest Global Pandemic: COVID-19

63. Lenny Bernstein and Jon Gerberg, "A Brooklyn ICU amid a Pandemic: Patients Alone, Comforted by Nurses and Doctors," *Washington Post*, April 4, 2020. www.washingtonpost.com.
64. Bernstein and Gerberg, "A Brooklyn ICU amid a Pandemic."
65. MacKenzie, *Covid-19*, p. xi.
66. Seema Yasmin and Craig Spencer, "'But I Saw It on Facebook': Hoaxes Are Making Doctors' Jobs Harder," *New York Times*, August 28, 2020. www.nytimes.com.
67. Quoted in Glenn Thrush, "'It Affects Virtually Nobody,' Trump Says, Minimizing the Effect of the Coronavirus on Young People as the U.S. Death Toll Hits 200,000," *New York Times*, September 22, 2020. https://www.nytimes.com.
68. Christian Paz, "All the President's Lies About the Coronavirus," *The Atlantic*, August 31, 2020. www.theatlantic.com.
69. Leslie Nemo, "Why People of Color Are Disproportionately Hit by COVID-19," *Discover*, June 12, 2020. www.discovermagazine.com.
70. Conniff, "How Pandemics Have Changed Us," p. 73.

For Further Research

Books

Charles River Editors, *The Antonine Plague: The History and Legacy of the Ancient Roman Empire's Worst Pandemic*. Independently published, 2020.

Barbara Krasner, *Pandemics and Outbreaks*. New York: Greenhaven, 2020.

Daisy Luther, *Be Ready for Anything: How to Survive Tornadoes, Earthquakes, Pandemics, Mass Shootings, Nuclear Disasters, and Other Life-Threatening Events*. New York: Racehorse, 2019.

Hal Marcovitz, *The Covid-19 Pandemic: The World Turned Upside Down*. San Diego, CA: ReferencePoint, 2021.

Jason McGill, *The Great Pandemics: Duration and Impacts with Eyewitness Accounts*. N.p.: Red Gazelle, 2020.

Frank M. Snowden, *Epidemics and Society: From the Black Death to the Present*. New Haven, CT: Yale University Press, 2019.

Internet Sources

Jared Aarons, "FDA Grants Emergency Approval for San Diego Company's COVID-19 Antibody Test," ABC 10 News San Diego, July 29, 2020. www.10news.com.

Angus Chen, "One of History's Worst Epidemics May Have Been Caused by a Common Microbe," *Science*, January 16, 2018. www.sciencemag.org.

Christine Hauser, "The Mask Slackers of 1918," *New York Times*, August 3, 2020. www.nytimes.com.

History, "Why Was It Called the Spanish Flu?," March 27, 2020. www.history.com.

Owen Jarus, "20 of the Worst Epidemics and Pandemics in History," Live Science, March 20, 2020. www.livescience.com.

Rebecca Jennings, "Coronavirus Is Making Us All Socially Awkward," Vox, July 17, 2020. www.vox.com.

Douglas Jordan, "The Deadliest Flu: The Complete Story of the Discovery and Reconstruction of the 1918 Pandemic Virus," Centers for Disease Control and Prevention, December 17, 2019. www.cdc.gov.

Andrew Joseph, "'A Huge Experiment': How the World Made So Much Progress on a Covid-19 Vaccine So Fast," STAT, July 30, 2020. www.statnews.com.

Geoffrey Migiro, "What Was the Antonine Plague?," WorldAtlas, January 30, 2020. www.worldatlas.com.

Michelle Roberts, "What Is Bubonic Plague?," BBC, 2020. www.bbc.com.

Dave Roos, "How 5 of History's Worst Pandemics Finally Ended," History, 2020. www.history.com.

Dave Roos, "Social Distancing and Quarantine Were Used in Medieval Times to Fight the Black Death," History, 2020. www.history.com.

World Health Organization, "Coronavirus Disease (COVID-19) Advice for the Public: Mythbusters," 2020. www.who.int.

Websites

COVID-19, US Department of Labor (www.osha.gov/SLTC /covid-19). This excellent site contains numerous links leading to a wide range of information about COVID-19, including medical facts, symptoms, control and prevention, how workers can avoid contracting the virus, the importance of wearing masks, and much more.

Pandemics That Changed History, History (www.history.com /topics/middle-ages/pandemics-timeline). This informative site presents an overview of many of history's largest disease outbreaks, including cholera, leprosy, measles, bubonic plague, and HIV/AIDS. The authors provide several links to several subarticles that cover related material.

Plague, World Health Organization (www.who.int/health-top ics/plague#tab=tab_1). The World Health organization compiled this collection of valuable information about bubonic plague's existence in the modern world and the steps that health professionals around the globe are taking to keep that dreaded disease in check.

Index

Picture Credits

About the Author

Classical historian, amateur astronomer, and award-winning author Don Nardo has written numerous volumes about medical and scientific topics, including *Technology and Medicine; Destined for Space* (winner of the Eugene M. Emme Award for best astronomical literature); *Tycho Brahe* (winner of the National Science Teacher's Association's best book of the year); *Planet Under Siege: Climate Change*; *Deadliest Dinosaurs*; and *The History of Science*. Nardo, who also composes and arranges orchestral music, lives with his wife, Christine, in Massachusetts.